Say it in Scots

SCOTTISH WILDLIFE

Say it in Scots

SCOTTISH WILDLIFE

Chris Robinson

BLACK & WHITE PUBLISHING

First published 2008
by Black & White Publishing Ltd
99 Giles Street, Edinburgh EH6 6BZ

ISBN: 978 1 84502 195 5

1 3 5 7 9 10 8 6 4 2   07 08 09 10 11

Copyright © Chris Robinson, 2008
Illustrations by Garry Thorburn
www.caricaturecards.co.uk

A CIP catalogue record for this book is available from the British Library.

Typeset by Ellipsis Books Ltd
Printed and bound by Nørhaven Paperbacks A/S

Contents

Say it in Scots   1

Introduction   3

1. Birds   6

2. Big Beasts   52

3. Wee Beasts   73

4. Freshwater Fish   85

5. Sea Life   90

6. Creepy Crawlies   102

Epilogue   121

Say it in Scots

Whether you are a Scots speaker already, or whether you are a visitor to Scotland, this series of books is guaranteed to awaken your enthusiasm for the Scots language. There is bound to be something in these books to interest you. They are based on the *Scottish National Dictionary* and *A Dictionary of the Older Scottish Tongue*, which are now available online as the *Dictionary of the Scots Language* at **www.dsl.ac.uk.** Additional material comes from the ongoing research of Scottish Language Dictionaries, who are responsible for the stewardship of these great reference works and for keeping the record of Scots words up to date.

Scots is the language of Lowland Scotland and the Northern Isles. It is also used in parts of Ulster. Along with English and Gaelic, it is one of Scotland's three indigenous languages. Scots is descended from Northern Old English, itself greatly influenced by Old

Scandinavian. From the twelfth century onwards, it became increasingly established in Lowland Scotland and was then enriched by words borrowed from French, Latin, Gaelic and Dutch. It was the language of state, spoken by kings, courtiers, poets and the people. It has a literary heritage the equal of any in Europe.

Like any other language, it has its own dialects such as Glaswegian, Ayrshire, Shetland, Doric, Border Scots, etc. These have a rich diversity and share a central core uniting them as varieties of the Scots language. We have tried to reflect the history and variety of Scots in these books and hope you will find some words that you can savour on your tongue and slip into everyday conversation.

Some of the spelling, especially in the older quotations, may be unfamiliar, but if you try reading the quotations out loud, you will find they are not difficult to understand.

Chris Robinson

Director

Scottish Language Dictionaries

www.scotsdictionaries.org.uk

Introduction

I'm truly sorry Man's dominion
Has broken Nature's social union,
An' justifies that ill opinion,
Which makes thee startle,
At me, thy poor, earth-born companion,
An' fellow-mortal!

(ROBERT BURNS *To a Mouse*)

Scotland is fortunate in that it provides a variety of habitats. There are rich arable lands, deciduous woodlands and pine forests, bleak bare mountains, lochs, tumbling streams and great rivers with wide shallow estuaries, peat bogs and cliffs, rocky and sandy coasts. Much of the land is still only sparsely inhabited, leaving undisturbed sites for some of the rarer species. This allows the country to support a great range of wildlife, some of which is absent from the rest of the UK. However, many of these environments are fragile, and the encroachment of man and domestic animals is an ever-present danger. Because it is sometimes difficult to draw the line between truly wild animals and feral animals, and because the land is often shared, some domestic and farmed animals and birds are included in this collection of wildlife words.

Scotland can be proud of her conservation record. One of the first Scots who understood the importance of conservation was John Muir, the pioneer of National Parks in the USA. Now there is a John Muir Country Park near his birthplace in Dunbar and the John Muir Trust undertakes a tremendous range of projects throughout the country.

This little book brings together many of the creatures that have inhabited Scotland. Some are no longer found within these shores and some of their names are dying out, for the language too is a living entity in danger and in need of conservation. Scottish Language Dictionaries are leaders in the conservation of the Scots Language. That said, Scots is still a vibrant and colourful language in which the wonders of nature, its lore and its legends can still be told.

1 Birds

Syne crownit scho the Egle king of fowlis,
And as steill dertis scherpit scho his pennis,
And bawd him be als just to awppis and owlis
As unto pacokkis, papingais or crennis,
And mak a law for wycht fowlis and for wrennis,
And lat no fowll of ravyne do efferay
Nor devoir birdis bot his awin prey.

[Then she (Dame Nature) crowned the Eagle king of birds, and as steel darts sharpened she his feathers, and bade him be as just to bullfinches and owls as to peacocks, parrots or cranes, and make one law for powerful birds and for wrens, and let no bird of prey cause alarm to or devour any birds except his own prey.]

This idealised medieval image of avian harmony and organisation is taken from *The Thrissill and the Rose*, written by William Dunbar to celebrate the marriage of James IV to Margaret Tudor, which took place on 8 August 1503. The eagle here represents King James, and Dame Nature is seen here as having a hand in bringing peace, justice and rightful order to Scotland.

Using birds and their characteristics to describe people is still common, but the likenesses are usually less flattering than the royal eagle. See **Corbie messenger**, **Gled** and **Gowk** for example.

Beardie – whitethroat *Sylvia communis*. Charles

Swainson describes its beard in *The Folk-Lore and Provincial Names of British Birds* (1885). *Its light-coloured head and neck feathers stand out more thickly than is usual in other birds.* See also **Blethering Tam**.

Black cock – the male of the Black Grouse *Tetrao tetrix*. The numbers of these fine birds with their dramatic courtship display are declining. A reason for the decline may be suggested by that fact that if you *make a black cock* of someone, you shoot them. This is illustrated in the account of Archibald Stewart's trial 1753:

> *He would make black cocks of them, before they entered into possession, by which the deponent understood shooting them*

and in Sir Walter Scott's *Waverley* (1814):

> *And I hae heard mae than ane say they wadna tak muckle to mak a black-cock o' ye.*

Black-throated diver – *Gavia arctica*. There are fewer than 200 breeding pairs in the UK, mainly in the lochs in the extreme north of Scotland, although there is a better chance of seeing them in winter along the Moray Firth and the north-west coast.

Blethering Tam – whitethroat *Sylvia communis*. The *Herald* (27 August 1994) describes it:

> *Ashy head, fawn-pink belly, ochre back and white outer tail feathers make the whitethroat easy to identify, quite apart from its eponymous field mark, which it often puffs out in display. Hence the old Scots name, Beardie, others being White Lintie and Blethering Tam, this last as much from its drinker's pose.*

Bonxie – great skua *Catharacta skua*.

Bubbly-Jock – turkey. The poet Hugh Macdiarmid described it as *hauf like a bird And hauf like a bogle*.

Burnbecker – see **Dipper.**

Capercailzie – woodgrouse *Tetrao urogallus*. Whether you pronounce the first syllable as *cap* or *cape* is up to you, but what you must not do is pronounce that *z*. It represents an old letter known as *yogh* which was pronounced like the first sound in *yes*, but in many cases it has now become silent. It is usually silent in capercailzie. The letter was originally written like an old-fashioned handwritten z and this is why printers used that letter shape for it, giving rise to all manner of confusion. Now we have the surname Menzies pronounced in two different ways. Older occasional spellings such as Mackenyie reveal that Mackenzie has changed its pronunciation. Another surname to watch out for is Dalziel.

Not only does the capercailzie have an interesting spelling, it also has an interesting derivation. It comes from the Gaelic *capull coille* meaning 'horse of the wood'. This is a reference to its considerable size. The male measures 33 inches and the female 25 inches.

John Leslie's 1596 translation of Dalrymple's *Historie of Scotland* explains:

> *A certane foul and verie rare called the capercalze*

*to name with the vulgar peple, the horse of the
forrest.*

We read that, in 1746, *Caperkellies are frequently sold
in mercat*, according to Kington Oliphant in *The Jacobite
Lairds of Gask* (published in 1870), but by 1760, Robert
Pococke notes in *Tours in Scotland*:

> *In the Mountain towards Fort Augustus they have
> found the Caper Keily (Cock of the Wood). They are
> now very rare. I saw the skin of one stuffed, they are
> about the size of a Turkey, the head like a Grouse
> or Moor Fowl, entirely black, except that the Belly is
> spotted with White, and it is white under the Wings.*

Soon after, the 1795 *Statistical Account* for Inverness
suggests that the species has become extinct in Scotland:

> *The caper coille, or wild turkey, was seen in
> Glenmoriston, and in the neighbouring district of
> Strathglass, about 40 years ago, and it is not known
> that this bird has appeared since, or that it now
> exists in Britain.*

It was reintroduced from Sweden in the late 1830s and, Archibald Rea asserts in *The Divot Dyke* (1898), the cock bird's distinctive voice was to be heard once again in the Scottish highlands:

> *The capercailzie up the glen Was churkin' loodly to his hen.*

This quotation does not quite do justice to the call which starts as a rattle and then sounds disconcertingly like the popping of a cork and pouring of liquid, ending with a harsh grinding noise.

Cleckin – the act of hatching; a brood or litter. An early awareness of conservation issues is shown in the following quotation from *The Acts of the Parliaments of Scotland* (1592):

> *The . . . solane geis being sua yeirlie slayne . . . ar maid vnhable to clek young birdis.*

The word is clearly used in the sense of litter of young in J. Christie's article in the *Banffshire Journal* (22 May 1906):

> *An' whaur's the cattie wi' her cleckin?*

and again in John Galt's Annals of the Parish (1821):
She had set her mind on a clecking of pigs.

In some areas cleckin is used exclusively of hatching eggs and there may be some overlap with **Clock**. For a *doo's cleckin* see **Doo**.

Chookie – chicken. There are two rare Scots breeds, the Scots Dumpy and the Scots Grey (not to be confused with the former Scots cavalry regiment). The dumpy, as the name suggests, is a short-legged breed, which comes in a variety of colours and provides good layers and good broody hens. The speckled Scots Grey, on the other hand, is less inclined to sit on eggs but lays big eggs for the size of the bird and its longer legs enable it to cope with rougher terrain. They are a particularly pretty breed.

Clock, *Cloak* – the cry or noise made by hens when they wish to sit on eggs for the purpose of hatching; to brood, sit on eggs, hatch.

Corbie – raven; carrion crow; rook. This is one of many Scots words of Old French origin, deriving from *corb* or *corbin*.

Although there is variation regarding which member of the crow family the word refers to, there are some quotations which make the writer's intention clear. The presence of large numbers of corbies in trees suggests a rookery in Seton Gordon's *Hill Birds of Scotland* (1915):

> D'ye ken the hoose o' Sir William Forbes,
> Surrounded by trees a' black wi' corbies.

By a process of elimination, we can infer that the following quotation from William Stewart's massive *Buik of the Croniclis of Scotland* (1535) uses corbie for the carrion crow:

> Baith ravin and ruik, with corbie, ka [jackdaw]
> and craw [hooded crow], Biggit nestis and eggis
> laid thairto;

but there is no doubt that the next quotation, from

Richard Holland's *The Book of the Howlat* (1452), refers to the raven, as we know from the story of Noah:

> *How, corby messingere, . . . Thow ischit owt of*
> *Noyes ark & to the erd wan* [reached land], *Taryit as*
> *a tratour and brocht na tythingis* [tidings].

The failure of the raven to return to the Ark has given us the phrase **corbie messenger** for any dilatory or unfaithful messenger.

Another common phrase is **a gone corbie** for a person who is beyond medical help:

> *At the lang hinner en' the doctor tell't . . . that he*
> *was a . . . gone corbie, an' that he would ha'e to*
> *put his hoose in order*

> (Joseph Waugh *Cute McCheyne* 1917)

The stepped coping of gables, characteristic of much fifteenth-century Scottish architecture, is known as **corbie steps**.

Most Scots school children know the sinister ballad of *The Twa Corbies*:

As I was walkin all alane,
I heard twa corbies makin mane;   (moan)
The tane untae the tither say,
"Whaur sal we gang and dine the day?"

"In ahint yon auld fail dyke,   (turf wall)
I wat there lies a new slain knight;
And naebody kens that he lies there
But his hawk, his hound, and lady fair."

"His hound is tae the huntin gane,
His hawk tae fetch the wild-fowl hame,
His lady's taen anither mate,
Sae we may mak oor dinner swate."

"Ye'll sit on his white hause-bane,   (collar bone)
And I'll pike out his bonny blue een;
Wi ae lock o his gowden hair
We'll theek oor nest an it growes bare."

"There's mony an ane for him maks mane,
But nane sal ken whaur he is gane;
Ower his white banes, whan they are bare,
The wind sall blaw for evermair."

The corbies may pick out the eyes of a knight, but there is a degree of honour among crows as among thieves, if the proverb cited by Andrew Henderson in *Scottish Proverbs* (1832) is true:

Corbies dinna pick out corbies' een.

$Craw$ – crow. In Scotland it is often applied to the rook and the hooded crow or **hoodie craw** as well as the carrion crow. A sixteenth-century saying warns of partiality:

The black craw thinks her ain bird whitest.

A later saying warns of consequences:

Whaur the craw flees her tail follows.

The Scots version of 'I have a bone to pick with you' is:
> *A hae a craw tae pluck wi ye.*

A craw in yer throat denotes a thirst especially one induced by an *excess of alcohol the night before.* A monumental hangover is described by James Smith in Habbie and Madge (1872):
> *For it's no a craw I'm fashed* [troubled] *wi' this mornin'; it's mair like an eagle or a vulture.*

For the Crow Road means about to die – a gone corbie!

Cushat, cushie doo – ring-dove or wood-pigeon *Columba palumbus.* Sir Walter Scott, in *The Lady of the Lake* (1810), alludes to the cushat in a typical literary way:
> *In answer coo'd the cushat dove Her notes of peace, and rest, and love.*

This legendary loving habit of doves means that the name of this bird and the sound it makes are often applied to affectionate human interactions:

I wad judge she's past the cooin', cushie-doo stage,
an' will sensibly consider this chance o' a guid
doon-settin'

(JOSEPH WAUGH Cute McCheyne 1917)

and:

O' Kirsty, jist say that you'll be mine, my bonnie
hen, my darlin' lamb, my ain wee cushie doo!

(ALEXANDER WARDROP Johnnie Mathison's
Courtship and Marriage 1881)

Who can say that the Scots are not romantic?

Dipper – dipper *Cinclus cinclus*. Also known as the **Water-craw** and the **Ess-cock** [waterfall-cock], the dipper is found in southern Europe, Scandinavia and parts of Asia, but is absent from the south of England. It is, however, a common sight in Scotland, working its way up burns [streams] and perching on rocks with its distinctive bobbing motion. This provides a vivid simile for James Hogg in *Dramatic Tales* (1817):

*The factor's naig wantit a fore-fit shoe, an' was
beckin* [nodding] *like a water-craw.*

It also gives the bird an alternative name in south-west
Scotland, **Burnbecker.**

The colouring of the dipper is described in the next
two quotations:

*See the jolly water-craw, A happy bird is he, Wi' a
collar roond his neck As white as white can be*

(THOMAS EDWARDS *Strathearn Lyrics* 1889)

*Water-craw, Water-craw, Coat o black and vest like
snaw.*

(J. K. ANNAND *Sing it Aince for Pleisure* 1965)

Doo – any species of pigeon. This is one bird that every
city-dweller knows:

*For a Clydebank waif whose contact with the
natural world among the sandstone canyons in the
1950s was restricted to scabby doos, scruffy cats,
three-legged dugs . . .*

(*Herald* 16 October 1999)

Like working men in many other parts of the British Isles, Scots, particularly in mining communities, enjoyed racing pigeons. These were treated like royalty. Davie Kerr demonstrates the high priority they had in men's lives in *A Puckle Poems* (2000):

Drookit miners at lowsin, whan hame fae the mine,
Suin stripp't aff thir pee-wee's [singlets]*, ti a scrub*
in the bine [wash tub]
Syne gaed doun ti thir doo-cots, ti let oot the
doos, . . .

For more information on pee-wees, see **Peesweep.**

The interesting derivative **doo's cleckin** comes from the pigeon's regular egg-laying regime:

When domesticated they [rock doves] *have four broods in the year, always two at a time – male and female. Hence a boy and girl* [i.e. twins] *are called 'a doo's cleckin''*

(GEORGE BRUCE *The Land Birds in and around St Andrews* 1895)

Earn – golden eagle *Aquila chrysaëtos*; the white-tailed or sea eagle *Haliaetus albicilla*. An early reference to the eagle is found in an Act of Parliament of 1457:

> *Foulys of reif* [prey, plunder] *as ernys, bussardis, gleddis, and myttallis . . .*

The majesty of the eagle is encapsulated in the idea of it being Jove's bird. This is a reference to the myth of Jupiter turning himself into an eagle in order to carry off Ganymede. Gavin Douglas's translation of the *Aeneid* (1513) contains this allusion:

> *Jovis fowle, the ern, com sorand by.*

The use of the word earn to describe two different birds is clearly evidenced in the next two quotations. The classification in the second of these is unusual, but it does seem to refer to the sea eagle.

> *The golden eagle used formerly to build in our rocks, though of late it has discontinued the practice . . . they are commonly known among the shepherds by the name of the earn, a visit of which*

amongst the flock is dreaded as much as that of the fox.

(Statistical Account 1795)

Here does the Eagle nest, and haunt, but it is not the Chrysaetos, but that sort called the Pygargus Hinnularius turneri, or the Ern

(ALEXANDER PENNECUIK A Geographical and Historical Description of the Shire of Tweeddale 1715)

Ess-cock – see **Dipper.**

Foul, fool – fowl, a bird of any kind but often a bird used as food.

Creatoure saw he nane . . . Nothyre fule, man, na beste.

(JOHN BARBOUR Legends of the Saints 1380)

Gled – the red kite *Milvus milvus*. This once common scavenger became extinct in Scotland in 1879 but reintroduction in 1989 means that this magnificent and distinctive bird can now be seen in increasing numbers and in increasingly widespread areas.

They make regular appearances in Scottish literature. In the *Flyting of Dunbar and Kennedy* (1508), a poetic exchange in which the two poets try to outdo each other in creative insults, Dunbar describes Kennedy as

Evill farit and dryit, . . . Lyke as the gleddis had on thy gule [yellow] *snowt dynd.*

The word was sometimes extended to include other birds such as the sparrow-hawk, the hen-harrier and the buzzard:

Both Kites and Hen Harriers were called Gleds, and so it is difficult to say which is meant in the old records . . . In Berwickshire, Hen Harriers were known as Grey Gleds, and Dr Harvey said he often saw Grey Gleds in Coldingham moor from 1820 to 1830

(L. J. Rintoul and E. V. Baxter *A Vertebrate Fauna of Forth* ed. 1935)

Robert Burns in *The Trogger* (1796) clearly means a buzzard:

Here is Satan's picture, Like a bizzard gled.

Frequently, gled has been used of people who possessed character traits associated with the raptor. Fortunately university education in Scotland has become less traumatic since 1868:

An' a' thae greedy gleds o' professors to pay, that live upo' the verra blude and banes o' sair-vroucht students!

(GEORGE MACDONALD *Robert Falconer* 1868)

Gled-wylie is a children's game in which one of the bigger children takes the part of the gled and tries to catch some of the smaller children or the 'chickens', who stand in a string protected by the 'mither-bird' at the head.

To be *as if ane had faen frae the gled* is to be dishevelled and confused, as if rescued or dropped from the claws of a bird of prey.

To be *in the gled's claws* or *grups* is to be in mortal danger, without chance of escape.

Goggie – a child's name for an egg; an unfledged bird, a nestling.

Gorb, gorbie, gorbet – an unfledged bird.

> *The gorbets, there's but three; An' sune they'll flap their little wings, An' try frae hame tae flee*
>
> (John Fullerton *Poems* 1905)

Clergymen are sometimes referred to as **God's gorbies** and John Galt makes it clear in *Literary Life and Miscellanies* (1834) that no lack of reverence is intended:

> *The clergy are God's gorbies, and for their Master's sake it behoves us to respect them.*

Gormaw – cormorant *Phalacrocorax carbo*.

Gowk – cuckoo *Cuculus canorus*. The Scots word gowk meaning 'cuckoo', from Old Norse *gaukr*, makes an early appearance in Scots literature, in the company of other birds, in William Dunbar's account in the *Fenyeit Friar* (c.1508) of an unfortunate fraud who attempted to fly with borrowed feathers:

The golk, the gormaw, and the gled,
Beft [beat] *him with buffettis quhill* [until] *he bled.*

The timing of the gowk's arrival, to coincide with changeable weather, has given rise to the expression **a gowk's storm**, meaning one of short duration. This was applied figuratively in a letter from the Earl of Huntly (1594), in which, Patrick Tytler's History of Scotland tells us,

he spoke of the King's rumoured campaign as likely to turn out a gowk's storm.

Gowk is often used to refer to a fool. A diary entry of Alexander Brodie of Brodie (1677) ruefully records:

My woful passion brok out, and I cald him a fool and gouk.

J. K. Annand's poem, *The Gowk*, illustrates this sense with gentle humour:

I met a gowk frae Penicuik
Wha thocht he was a bird;
The wey he flaffed and cried "Cuckoo",
He lookit fair absurd.
Whit wey he thinks he is a bird,
I haena got a clue;
But tho he's no a feathered gowk,
There's nae dout he's cuckoo.

The link between gowks and the first of April is well documented; from 1840 we have an example in Andrew Henderson's collection, *A Few Rare Proverbs*:

The first day of April, send the gowk anither mile,
and we all have childhood memories of queer, daft-
like, wonderful errands . . . that . . . Gowks were
occasionally sent on.

(*Kelso Chronicle* 3 April 1925)

The practice is widely known as **hunt-the-gowk** or

huntegowk and the degree of Noah's trust in his God is amply shown where Noah sets to work building the ark,

> *kennin' fine that the Lord wouldna gi'e him a hunty-gowk*

(MARSHALL BELL Pickles and Ploys 1932)

Gwalock – snow bunting *Plectrophenax nivalis*. A winter visitor, although there are a few breeding pairs in Scotland. This name is a corruption of Gaelic *gealag* meaning 'a little white thing'.

Heather-bleet – snipe *Gallinago gallinago*.

Hoodie craw – see **Craw**.

Howtowdie – a large chicken for the pot (a bird for the gourmet rather than the ornithologist); a young hen which has not begun to lay; (figuratively) an unmarried woman.

This mouthwatering suggestion from Elizabeth

Cleland's *A New and Easy Method of Cookery* (1759) makes a change from the common Scottish stuffing of fried onions and oatmeal:

> *Chickens farced with Oisters . . . You may do*
> *Howtoudies or any white Fowl, the same way.*

And a recipe for romance:

> *Doun below this auld howtowdie lived a*
> *superannuated patriarchal widower.*

(JAMES SMITH *Canty Jock* 1882)

And here is a picture of connubial harmony:

> *Chanticleer* [name for a cock], *sae fu' o'*
> *pride . . . Wi's hen and 'toudies by his side*

(R. BROWN *Lintoun Green* 1817)

Houlet, howlet, hoolet – (all pronounced with an *oo* as in *hoot*) owl. The **horned houlet** is the long-eared owl *Asio otus*; the **Jenny houlet** is the tawny owl *Strix aluco sylvatica*; and the **white houlet** is the barn owl, *Tyto alba*.

It is not unusual to see an owl being mobbed by other birds: Than fleis thow, lyk ane howlat chest with [chased by] *crawis;*

(WALTER KENNEDY *The Flyting of Dunbar and Kennedy* 1508)

An interesting observation occurs in Bellenden's translation of *The Chronicles of Scotland* by Hector Boece (1531):

Ane sparhalk wes strangulat be ane howlat.

Houlets in Scottish literature and lore are not regarded as benevolent and wise owls like English owls. Instead, they are treated with suspicion, as birds of darkness, and so to liken someone to an owl is to hold them in low esteem. There are many examples of such choice insults:

The said Johnne being ane fugitiue and ane howlat, nocht appearand in the day.

(ROBERT PITCAIRN *Ancient Criminal Trials in Scotland* 1618)

Calling her ill-faced houlett, lyk that catt, thy sister . . .

> *(The Register of the Privy Council of Scotland 1663)*

It issued in the question of fact as to whether said schoolmaster had called an elder or fellow Christian a cur carle [miser, old man, low fellow], or souters [shoemaker's] houlet

> (Adam Ritchie *The Churches of Saint Baldred: Auldhame, Whitekirk, Tyninghame, Prestonkirk* 1700 in 1880 edition)

Let howlet Whigs do what they can, The Stuarts will be back again.

> *(Jacobite Minstrelsy 1715)*

Kae – jackdaw *Corvus monedula*. The jackdaw, like many scavengers, is often associated with misfortune:

> *The gret kirk of Sanctandros . . . was brynt . . . be ane ka . . . bering ane spark of fire to hir nest;*

> (John Bellenden *The Chronicles of Scotland, compiled by Hector Boece* 1531)

They were even associated with witchcraft, as in this strange confession recorded in Pitcairn's *Ancient Criminal Trials in Scotland* (1662):

> *I* [Isobel Gowdie] *went in, in the likenes of a kea and the said Elspet Chisolm wes in the shape of a catt.*

Laverock, larick – skylark *Alauda arvensis*. Any frivolous objection to a suggestion may be countered with

> *Ay, an the sky'll fa and smoor* [smother] *the laverocks.*

Another saying, quoted in Andrew Henderson *Scottish Proverbs* (1832), praising someone's persuasive powers is:

> *You wad wheedle a laverock frae the lift.*

On a cold and stormy night, you might look wisely at the sky and say:

> *There's nae reek* [smoke] *ee laverock's house the nicht.*

> (L. WILSON *Lowland Scotch as spoken in the Lower Strathearn District* 1915)

Can you solve this riddle, posed in John MacTaggart's *The Scottish Gallovidian Encyclopedia* (1824)? You will find the answer and explanation at the end of the book.

The laverock and the lark, The bawkie and the bat,
The heather-bleet, the mire-snipe, How many burds
be that?

An uncommon but pretty name for bog cotton is **laverock's lint.**

Lintie, lintwhite – linnet *Acanthis cannabina.* This gregarious little bird has a number of different names. These may derive from its appearance, like **rose lintie** from the red breast of the male. **Whin-lintie** refers to its habitat, as it likes to nest among gorse bushes. The word lintie itself comes from the lint seeds on which it feeds and, in lintwhite, this is combined with an onomatopoeic representation of its alarm call. Samuel Smiles in *Life of a Scotch Naturalist* (1876) adds, for the confusion of the bird-watcher:

It is the rose lintie so long as it retains its red

breast; but when that is gone or wanting, it is then the gray lintie, the whin lintie, the brown lintie, and so on.

The lintie is known for its song and *singin like a lintie* is a common simile and one used by Raymond Vettese in *The Richt Noise* (1988):

I'm gleg [lively] *as a flech* [flea], *spinnin like a peerie* [top], *singin like a lintie an' oh, I canna weary.*

To beat bushes for linties is to be employed on some useless or unprofitable task:

I'll be paid for my trouble. I dinna gang about beating bushes for linties

(*Blackwood's Magazine* October 1826)

Loom – red-throated diver or rain-goose *Colymbus stellatus*, or the great northern diver, *Colymbus immer*.

Marrot – razorbill *Alca torda*; guillemot *Uria aalge*. As Rintoul and Baxter point out in their *Vertebrate Fauna of*

Forth (1935), there is a great deal of confusion in bird names:

> It is unfortunate that the old names Marrot and Scout referred to both Razorbills and Guillemots.

Mavis – song thrush *Turdus philomelos*.

Maw – gull.

Mitten, mittan(e), myttal – probably the male hen-harrier *Circus cyaneus*.

Osprey – osprey *Pandion haliaetus*. The return of the osprey to Scottish lochs is a conservation success story. In spite of setbacks caused by theft of osprey eggs, numbers are increasing and these magnificent birds can be seen plunging into the water and emerging with a fish in their talons at Loch Garten, the Loch of the Lowes and a gradually increasing number of sites throughout Scotland.

Pairtrick – partridge *Perdix perdix*. This little bird makes a good dinner:

> The airn and the goshalk syne, That dentely had
> wont to dyne, On pairtrick and on pliuer

> (JOHN BUREL *The Passage of the Pilgremer* 1590)

Papingo – parrot; popinjay. The parrot is not native to Scotland and does not survive long in the wild here, but it plays a large part in customs and heraldry. An entry in the Treasurer's Accounts (*Compota thesaurariorum Regum Scotorum* 1538) values King James V's parrot at ten crowns:

> To by ane papingo to the Kingis grace x cronis.

The arms of the Abercromby family consist of

> Three papingoes, vert [green], beaked and
> membered gules

> (*Burke's Peerage* 1959)

Membered means that the legs of the birds are a different colour from the rest of them. In this case the green birds had red legs.

The papingo or popinjay was used for archery practice and competitions:

The popingoe is a bird known in heraldry. It is . . . cut out in wood, fixed in the end of a pole, and placed 120 feet high, on the steeple of the monastery [at Kilwinning]. The archer who shoots down this mark, is honoured with the title of Captain of the Popingoe. He is master of the ceremonies of the succeeding year, sends cards of invitation to the ladies, gives them a ball and supper, and transmits his honours to posterity by a medal, with suitable devices, appended to a silver arrow

(Statistical Account 1795)

Also:

On Saturday last the Papingo Prize of the Royal Company of Archers, Queen's Body Guard for Scotland, was shot for in the Butts at Archers' Hall

(Scotsman 18 February 1861)

Peesweep, peeweet, peewit, peezie, etc. – the lapwing *Vanellus vanellus*. In spite of its good work in eating harmful insects, the lapwing is not universally popular:

> *In the south of Scotland, this bird is termed*
> *the peesweep. In the south and west of Scotland,*
> *it is much detested, though not reckoned*
> *ominous*

(JOHN LEYDEN The Complaynt of Scotland 1801)

Sir Walter Scott suggests a reason for this in *Tales of a Grandfather (1829)*:

> *[The Covenanters] expressed great dislike of that*
> *beautiful bird, the Green-plover, in Scottish called*
> *the Peeseweep. The reason alleged was, that these*
> *birds being, by some instinct, led to attend to and*
> *watch any human beings whom they see in their*
> *native wilds, the soldiers were often guided in*
> *pursuit of the wanderers . . . by the plover being*
> *observed to hover over a particular spot.*

The melancholy cry, from which its name comes, may be another reason:

> *The teuchat was followed as it wailed out in circles*
> *round the intruder, "Peese-weet, peese-weet, hairy*
> *[harry] my nest, and gar me greet [make me weep]"*
>
> (Philosophical Society of Glasgow, *Proceedings* 1899)

A **peesweep storm** is a gale or snowstorm in the early spring, about the time the lapwings begin to pair.

Human beings who are compared to peesweeps are generally sharp-featured, gaunt, shrill-voiced, shrewish, whining, complaining, peevish or ailing:

> *Ony peesie-weesie, close-handit, peer-hairtit,*
> *nairrow-sowled coonterfeit in Gweed's creation . . .*
>
> (James Brown The Round Table Club 1873)

> *Come back oot o' there, you peeseweep-lookin'*
> *thing ye!*
>
> (Alexander Wardrop *Johnnie Mathison's*
> *Courtship and Marriage* 1881)

Or they might be an empty-headed, vain person, loud-voiced and showy:

> *Go, go, ye painted pisweips to fairs and waddins*
> [weddings], *and there display your proud banners*
> *of pride.*

(D<small>OUGAL</small> G<small>RAHAM</small> Collected Writings 1779)

A miner's singlet, of blue-grey flannel, like a lapwing's wings is also known as a peesweep.

See also **Teuchat.**

Pickmaw – black-headed gull *Larus ridibundus*.
> *The lav'rock, the peasweep, and skirlin' pickmaw,*
> *Shall hiss the bleak winter to Lapland awa*

(A<small>LEXANDER</small> S<small>COTT</small> Poems 1811)

Plivver – plover. The **gray plivver** refers to the knot *Calidris canutus*, while the **hill plivver** is the golden plover *Pluvialis apricarius*

Plivver's page – dunlin *Calidris alpina*. Alfred Smith reports in *Birds of Wiltshire* (1887):

> It is . . . said that a solitary Dunlin will attach itself to a solitary Golden Plover: and this strange notion has extended to the Hebrides, where from its habit of associating with those birds, it is called the 'Plover's Page'.

Ptarmigan, tarmigan – ptarmigan *Lagopus mutus*. This bird of the grouse family inhabits the northern parts of Scotland. It turns white in winter. While familiar to hillwalkers, it is rarely seen by less energetic bird watchers. Fortunately, it no longer appears on dinner tables although the prices given in the *Edinburgh Burgh Records* of 1668 suggest it was a luxury dish then:

> Tabell of the vivers [foodstuffs] in the pultrie mercat . . . the best termigant, 5 s.; drest, 6 s. 8 d.

Pyot – magpie *Pica pica*. The magpie is often perceived as a bird of ill-omen:

"A pyat! That's an ill sign," she said.

(ROBERT MACKENNA *Through Flood and Fire* 1925)

Still more ominous was the 'peat' when it appeared with one or three companions. An old rhyme about this bird runs "One is joy, two is grief, Three's a bridal, four is death"

(J. M. BARRIE *Auld Licht Idylls* 1888)

Given the uneasy relationship of the Clan Campbell with some of the other Scottish clans, there may also be a sense of the unwelcome messenger in the expression:

The pyet . . . is called 'the messenger of the Campbells'

(JOHN CAMPBELL *Superstitions of the Highlands and Islands* 1900)

Where English has the tell-tale-tit, Scots has the **tale-pyot** or **clash-pyot** as used by Sir Walter Scott in *The Antiquary* (1816):

I am no talepyet; but there are mair een in the
world than mine.

The reaction to telling tales may depend on whether
one is an authority figure or a member of a peer group
amongst whom solidarity is a matter of honour. Ian
MacLaren shows the teacher's ambiguous feelings
towards an informant in *Young Barbarians* (1901):

He hated a 'tell-pyet,' and yet knew that discipline
must be maintained.

But clypes (as tale-pyots are perhaps more often called in
Scotland) take note; in Samuel Crockett's *The Smugglers*
(1911):

The tongues of 'tale-pyets', or tellers of tales, were
scraped ungently with a piece of broken slate, and
thereafter washed.

An early example of tale-telling, recounted by Jean
White in *Moss Road* (1932), took place in the Garden
of Eden, when

*That gabbin' pyot, Adam, clypit to the Almighty
about Eve.*

See also **Kae.**

Rose Lintie – see **Lintie**.

Sanct Martinys fowle, Saint Martin's fowl –
probably the hen-harrier *Circus cyaneus.*
    William Dunbar's *The Fenyeit Friar* (1508) provides
a whole flock of bird quotations:
    *The myttane, and Sanct Martynis fowle, Wend he
    had bene the hornit howle* [long-eared owl].

Scorie – seagull.

Scottish crossbill – *loxia scotica.*

Scout – guillemot *Uria aalge.* John Leslie Bishop of
Ross, in his *Historie of Scotland* translated by Father
James Dalrymple in 1596, describes

*Ane certane kynd of fowle, in our mother toung
named the skout . . . in quantitie lytle mair than
the duke bot weil lang in body, sche layis her
egs gretter than guse-egs. In gret diligate is sche
haldne, . . . being sodin sche is maist tendir.*

[A certain kind of bird, in our mother tongue
named the scout . . . in size little more than the
duck but very long in the body, she lays her
eggs bigger than goose eggs. She is considered
a great delicacy . . . being boiled, she is most
tender.]

Sea Eagle – sea eagle *Haliaeetus albicilla*. The white-tailed sea eagle is the fourth largest eagle with a wingspan of over eight feet. Virtually extinct for a century, they are being reintroduced and are gradually becoming established in the West Highlands and the Inner Hebrides.

Shilfa, shilly – chaffinch *Fringilla caelebs*. In order to observe this ubiquitous and attractive little bird, all you have to do is open your picnic basket. Ornithologists will tell you it feeds on seeds and beech mast, but it does not avert its beak from sandwiches and cake.

It is also known as the **spink** and in this form it appears as a term of abuse in the vituperative *Flyting of Dunbar and Kennedy* (1508) when Kennedy addresses his antagonist:

> *Tale tellare, rebellare, induellar wyth the devillis,*
> *Spynk, sink wyth stynk ad Tertara termagorum.*

Skarf, scart – cormorant *Phalacrocorax carbo. To beat (the) scarfs* is to flap the arms against the sides to keep oneself warm on a cold day, like a cormorant flapping its wings.

Shetland is a wonderful place for seabirds. John Brand's observation in *The Description of the Countrey of Zetland* (1701) should have the twitchers heading north:

> *The Fowls have their Nests on the Holms in a very beautiful order . . . as the Scarfs by themselves, so*

the Cetywaicks [kittiwakes], *Tominories* [puffins], *Mawes* [gulls], *etc.*

Snawie, snawie-fuil – snow bunting. See **Gwalock.**

Solan goose – gannet *Morus bassanus.*

Sparhalk – (obsolete) the sparrowhawk *Accipiter nisus.* At a mere three shillings, the sparhalk was a lot less costly than a papingo:

Gevin to a man . . . that brocht a spar halk to the King iij s.

(*Compota thesaurariorum Regum Scotorum* 1473)

This seems a very reasonable amount for such a spirited hunter, capable of providing a good meal:

[He] *slew 6 partridges with a spar hauke*

(John Erskine *Journal of the Hon. John Erskine of Carnock* 1683)

Of course there was the additional cost of equipment and

again this is duly noted in the *Compota thesaurariorum Regum Scotorum* (1587):

Tua dosane of spar halk bellis L s. [50 shillings].

Spink – see **Shilfa.**

Spurg, sprug, speug – house sparrow *Passer domesticus.* William Milne in *Eppie Elrick* (1955) suggests that sparrow-legged men do not look good in the kilt:

Spurgie-hocht mennies dinna set 'e kilt.

Stuckie – starling *Sturnus vulgaris.* Roosting starlings reach plague-like proportions in cities from time to time as the *Scotsman* (6 February 1988) shows:

Not having any idea of the cloud due to arrive in
about 20 minutes he said: "So the hawks help tae
keep the stuckies doon?" In reply I quoted him
the old Scots saying: "Every drop helps" quoth the
wren when she pished in the sea.

Tammie Norie – puffin *Fratercula arctica.*

Teistie – guillemot *Uria aalge*.

Teuchat, teuchit – lapwing *Vanellus cristatus*. Their untidy flight is described in a poem by James Guthrie (1879):

> *The teuchats flaffer owre the tufftit bog.*

Tae hunt the teuchit is to be engaged on some fruitless pursuit and *a place the teuchits dinna ken o* is a very remote place, the back of beyond.

Throstle – song thrush *Turdus ericetorum*.

Water-craw – see **Dipper**.

Whaup – curlew *Numenius arquata*.

Whin-lintie – see **Lintie**.

Yella lintie, yite, yalla yite, yoldrin – yellow-hammer *Emberiza citrinella*. The yellow-hammer in England may sing 'a little bit of bread and no cheese' but Scottish ones are said to repeat *deil* [devil], *deil, deil tak ye*.

Hew Ainslie, in *A Pilgrimage to the Land of Burns* (1822), recalls an old superstition:

I never dream o' yites, but I meet auld frien's.

The diminutive form *yolty* is a nickname for a first-year student at Aberdeen University. Bajan or bejan (bec jaune or yellow beak) is a name for first years in several Scottish Universities:

He no longer allows the evil-minded fry on the
streets to insult his hat, or tug the yolty's gown with
impuniyt

(*Tait's Magazine* May 1833)

The quotations above show birds, not only on their natural habitat, but also in literature, heraldry and folklore. Perhaps more than any other creature, they catch the imagination and take the mind soaring in flights of fancy. The next chapter is more down to earth, but not without its own poetry, recipes and an interesting cure for a cough.

2 Big Beasts

A-chasing the wild deer and following the Roe
My heart's in the Highlands wherever I go.

(ROBERT BURNS)

Robert Burns was more renowned for chasing women than chasing deer, but the romance of deer-stalking still brings many visitors to the Highlands of Scotland where, in addition to the great Red Deer, portrayed in Landseer's painting as *The Monarch of the Glen*, there are plenty of wild and semi-wild animals to look out for.

Baver – beaver. There were beavers in Scotland until the sixteenth century and we find them listed in Bellenden's translation of Boece's *Chronicles of Scotland* (1531) with other indigenous animals:

> *mony martrikis, bevers, quhitredis, and toddis*

> [many pine martens, beavers, polecats (or other mustelidae) and foxes.]

There has been some discussion about the reintroduction of the European beaver to Scotland.

Brock – badger. There are many place-names (such as Broxburn and Broxden) which have brock, in some form, as an element, testifying to the wide distribution of these animals. In spite of being a retiring and charming animal, brock is often used as an insult, sometimes in reference to their tendency to smell. One of the dogs in Burns' poem *The Twa Dugs* (1786) compares the attitude of the upper classes to the poor with his own contempt of bagders:

> *They gang as saucy by poor folk, As I wad by a stinkan brock.*

According to Robert Henryson, *Bayth the bellox of ane brok . . . Is gud for the host* [cough]. However, if a badger's testicles are not available, you could try a hot whisky with honey and lemon instead.

Brockit – means coloured or striped like a badger. Cows, sheep and even cats can be described as brockit. A brockit-faced sheep has a white line down its nose. When used of a person, it means streaked with dirt.

Broket – a stag of the second year with straight single horns.

Caber – in case you thought a caber was just a great log, tossed at Highland Games, it can also mean one of the main antlers of a stag. Its derivative, **caberslash**, is a deer with unbranched antlers.

Cattle – the breed of cattle most often associated with Scotland is the photogenic Highland cow, with its great horns, tousled fringe and usually benign expression. Because of their hardiness and wonderfully lean and tasty meat, Highland cattle are becoming increasingly popular with smaller breeders. **Coo candy** is a colloquial name for a kind of toffee bar, so called from the highland cow on the wrapper.

There are other Scottish breeds which are not doing quite so well. The Shetland breed is struggling to increase its numbers, although it is a genuinely all-purpose beast, once used for draught as well as for milk and suckling calves for beef. Pretty little cows with short horns, they generally come in black and white or brown and white. Even the brown and white Ayrshire, once the ubiquitous milk cow on Scottish farms, has been to some extent ousted by breeds with less awkward horns, in spite of her good quality milk and delightful personality.

Even the well-known Aberdeen Angus, famous for its succulent marbled meat and exported to breeders in many countries, is less common at home owing to the increase in the use of larger, faster-maturing European breeds for beef production.

The ancient belted Galloway, originating from south west Scotland, with its highly distinctive broad white stripe around its middle, is increasing in popularity among beef producers. Hardy and hornless, these animals keep warm in winter by growing a thicker coat rather than by laying down fat.

Collie – this is defined with some affection in the *Scottish National Dictionary* as:

The Scottish sheep-dog, remarkable for its sagacity.

According to Sir Walter Scott, in *Waverley* (1817):

A French tourist . . . has recorded, as one of the memorabilia of Caledonia, that the state maintained in each village a relay of curs, called collies, whose duty it was to chase the chevaux de poste (too

starved and exhausted to move without such a
stimulus) from one hamlet to another.

I personally know of a descendant of such collies, which spent its prematurely curtailed life rounding up motor vehicles and trying to persuade them to proceed along the main street in the direction of its choice.

If someone says to you *Collie, wull ye lick* or *Collie wull ye taste*, interpret this as an invitation to partake of food. Unfortunately, this phrase more often appears in the negative:

I've sat whole nichts in their hooses an they never
so much as said to me, "Collie, wull ye lick?"

(O. Douglas *Ann and her Mother* 1922)

This inhospitable behaviour did not daunt a certain bishop, as David Calderwood records in *The History of the Kirk of Scotland* (1651):

The Bishop was nicknamed Collie, because he was
so impudent and shameless, that when the Lords
of the Session and Advocates went to dinner, he

*was not ashamed to follow them into their houses,
unasked, and sat down at their table.*

Clydesdale – this heavy horse, with his feathered, soup-plate feet and kind eyes, is a real gentle giant. Clydesdales come in a variety of colours but usually with a good admixture of white. Originally bred from Flemish stallions out of native Clydesdale mares, the breed today is aristocratic with an elegant action and a proud bearing. They were the pride and joy of horsemen on Scottish farms, dray horses in the cities, artillery horses in the mud of Flanders and the power behind the early days of forestry. Crossed with lighter breeds, they make rather wide-backed but otherwise comfortable and well-mannered, intelligent saddle horses.

Cuddy – donkey. This beast of burden, unfairly criticised for lack of intelligence, has lent its name to many pithy sayings, among them:

A cuddy should never handle tocher [money]

and:

> *A cuddy's gallop is soon done.*

Cuddy is sometimes used of a horse or pony. It is also used of a sawing-horse. There is a traditional riddle, the answer to which is at the end of this book:

> Hey-up ma cuddy, ma cuddy's ower the dyke [over the wall], and if ye meddle ma cuddy, ma cuddy'll gie ye a bite.

Deer – this animal needs a whole dictionary to itself. As a source of food and as the animal hunted by the nobility, it has become surrounded by technical terms and protocol.

See **Broket, Caber, Gralloch, Heavier, Hert, Hummel, Knobber, Mull, Ra, Red deer, Stag, Staggle, Ostoun**.

Dug – dog.

Gait, goat – goat. Wild goats are found in remote areas of the Scottish Highlands. They are the descendants of domestic goats but are now completely feral. A gait berry is an old name for the blackberry (in Scots, *bramble*) and hence the bramble bush was known as the gait tree.

Gralloch – the entrails of a deer; to remove the entrails.

Grice – a young pig. Grice has been used in the past to refer to a woman of ungraceful proportions and doubtful character. As these are almost unknown in Scotland, this usage has died out.

If you *bring the heid o the soo* [sow] *tae the tail o the grice,* you balance your loss with your gain.

Heavier – an ox-deer, a sexually undeveloped male deer, which generally grows to a greater size and weight than the normal animal.

Hert – hart, stag, male deer in his sixth year or older. An early account of hunting in Scotland is given in Bellenden's translation of Boece's *Chronicles of Scotland* (1531):

The Pichtis . . . drave the hertis apone the nettis
with thair hundis
[The Picts drove the harts upon the nets with their hounds.]

Horse – according to the *Transactions of the Banffshire Field Club* (1887):

A man who rode a piebald horse was believed
to have the privilege of prescribing for whooping
cough. Whatever remedy he recommended was
sure to be effectual. One such rider I have heard
of who seems to have been a rather ill-conditioned
individual, for when assailed with the usual formula
– "Man on the piet horse fat's guid for the kinkhost?"
he used to snappishly reply "butter an' bear caff"
[Man on the piebald horse what's good for whooping-cough? . . . Butter and barley chaff].

Hummel – with no antlers or horns, used of cattle or deer.

Kelpie – water horse. Like the **Loch Ness Monster**, this is a beast unknown to science, shrouded in mystery and speculation. It is, however, reputed to be dangerous. So, if a beautiful grey pony with a dripping wet mane appears, as you stand beside a quiet loch or river, do not be tempted to leap on its back, as there is no telling where it might take you.

Knobber – a young deer in his second year.

Loch Ness Monster – Nessie exists to boost the sale of T-shirts, soft toys and other souvenirs to the great benefit of the Scottish economy. Believed to favour the deep water close to the romantic Urquhart Castle, she is a rumour that refuses to go away. There is no smoke without fire! Or, to use the Scots expression for the same sentiment, *there is aye watter whaur the stirkie* [bullock] *droons.*

Mull – (of cattle or deer) without horns or antlers.

Oof, wolf – wolf. It is believed that the last wolf in Scotland was shot in 1743 and the Wolf Stone at Brora in Sutherland commemorates the event. There has been some debate about reintroducing the wolf to control the expanding red deer population but this is unlikely to happen.

Ostoun – a name for a stag of the fourth year.

Otter – this is found not just in the great salmon rivers of Scotland but also, along with lions, bears, stags, popinjays and griffons, in heraldry. One particular shield is described by Sir David Lindsay in *The Historie and Testament of Squyer Meldrum* (1550):

> *The squyer buir, into his scheild, Ane otter in ane siluer feild.*

Powny – pony. The small hardy Scottish breeds were invaluable to crofters for carrying loads and even for ploughing, driving and riding. Larger Highland ponies are a real all-purpose breed used for everything from bringing deer carcases off the hills to taking holidaymakers trekking to out-of-the-way places. They are a very comfortable ride and usually very well behaved. A small population of little grey Eriskay ponies are all that remains of the ponies that used to be widespread throughout the Western Isles. See also **Shelt.**

Puggie – monkey. Pugs, or more commonly puggies, did not seem to inspire affection and were a byword for ugliness. So we can assume the writer of the article in the *St Andrews Gazette* of 25 July 1862 was not a member of the temperance movement:

> *I'd faur rather crack nitts* [nuts] *a lee-lang winter's nicht wi' a puggy, than hear intemperate an' inconsistent speeches on temperance.*

Alan Ramsay speculates in verse (1722) that

> *'Tis Gowd that makes some great Men witty, And puggy Lasses fair and pretty.*

Another example of puggie being used pejoratively is given by James Stewart in his *Sketches of Scottish Character* (1857):

A skrankie [scraggy] *puggie face an' scaud ee*
[scabby eye].

Pugginess does not necessarily preclude affection, though,
as we read in Robert Louis Stevenson's *Catriona* (1893) of
My affection for my king, God bless the puggy face
of him.

A Scots speaker from Fife (1952) colourfully explained:
A person working clumsily with a tool is like a
puggy suppin pheesic [medicine] *wi' an elsin* [awl].

As fou as a puggie means extremely drunk.

Ra, roe deer – roe deer. The obsolete form, 'ra',
compounded with 'fell', an old word for skin to give **raffell**,
provides a word which appears in many old quotations,
showing how useful roe skin was. In the sixteenth-century
poem *Christis Kirk on the Grene* we read:
Thair gluvis wes of the raffell rycht.

The Household Book of Lady Grizell Baillie (1702) contains an entry for payment for a reffile for herpsicords. There are also various references to the use of roe skin for making laces.

Red deer – there are many herds of red deer in Scotland and their numbers are growing, to the detriment of natural woodland. They are increasingly being farmed for their low-cholesterol venison.

Reindeer – a small herd has been introduced in the Cairngorms where they do well in the tundra-like terrain.

Sanglere, sangleir, sanglar – wild boar. These animals have recently been reintroduced to parts of Scotland in the hope that they will control the growth of bracken and prepare the ground for the regeneration of native woodland. Let's hope that these do not fit the description that Adam Loutfut gives in his manuscript of 1494:

The sanglier . . . is callit in sum placis porc and

*othir sum sanglier. First he is richt ferce wnclene &
ennuyse* [malicious] *best* [beast].

Sheep – there are a number of famous breeds in Scotland.
The hardy Scottish Blackface and the Cheviot patrol the
hills in great numbers. Among the oldest and rarest sheep
are the North Ronaldsay sheep in Orkney, which have a
diet of seaweed for most of the year. They come in grey,
black and a reddish-brown colour which the Orcadians
call *moorit*. They have been shown to be related to the
sheep remains found at Skara Brae, an archaeological site
dating from 3000BCE. The rare Soay sheep, another of the
most primitive types of domestic sheep, are found wild
in St Kilda, the archipelago from which the last human
residents were evacuated in 1932. Even when the islands
were inhabited, the St Kildans had their own flocks which
were separate from the wild sheep. Soay sheep take their
name from the island of Soay in the St Kilda archipelago.
The name Soay actually means 'Sheep Island' in Old Norse,
which suggests the breed dates at least from Viking times.

Shelt – the tiny Shetland pony is popular as a pet and as a child's first pony although it can exhibit a kind of self-opinionated obstinacy, best translated by the Scots word *thrawn,* and most of them have a quirky sense of humour. Shelt is occasionally used of any pony.

Stag – a male deer in his sixth year or older.

Staggle – a male deer in his third year

Stirk – a bullock or heifer between one and two years old.

Tod – fox. The fox has long been synonymous with cunning and treachery and there are many fables and proverbs based on these attributes. A very strange saying comes from the collection of James Carmichael (died 1628):

> *It wilbe a gude fyre quhen it burns, it is beginnand*
> *to reik, as the tod said quhen he schete on the yse.*

[It will be a good fire when it burns, it is beginning to smoke, as the fox said when he shat on the ice.]

Do not go building theories on misleading evidence!

Farmers have always sought to justify the hunting of foxes on the grounds of the damage that they do in the henhouse. Perhaps they should try the preventative measures described by Boece in his *Chronicles of Scotland*, translated by John Bellenden (1531):

Ilk hous of this cuntre, nurisis ane young tod
certane dayis, and mengis the flesche thairof, eftir
that it be slane, with sic meit as thay gif to thair
fowlis, or uthir smal beistis; and sa mony as etis
of this meit ar preservit twa monethis eftir fra ony
dammage of toddis, for toddis will eit na flesche
that gustis of thair awin kind.

[Every house of this country nourishes a young fox for several days and mixes its flesh, after it is killed, with such food as they give to their poultry, or other small animals, and all those that eat this food are protected for two months after from any harm from foxes, for foxes will eat no flesh that tastes of their own kind.]

No source of heat was wasted in pre-central-heating days. If you ever wanted to know how a king kept warm in bed, the answer is supplied in an entry for 1522 in the Accounts of the Treasurer of Scotland:

Item, for ane lynying of tod powtis to the kingis nichtgoun of chamelot viij li. v s

[Item, for a lining of fox pelt for the king's nightgown of chamlet eight pounds five shillings.]

Camlet is a kind of fine eastern fabric originally of silk and goat hair.

Wild cat – these elusive forest-dwellers are in many ways similar to the domestic tabby, which is probably descended from them. They are larger than the domestic cat, with stubby tails, but, although the wild cat is monogamous, there has been interbreeding with unscrupulous domestic cats, which means that there is increasing hybridisation except in the most remote areas. You are certainly not going to see one such as Sir Gilbert Hay describes in *The Buik of King Alexander the Conquerour* (1460):

> *Thare wyld cattis ar grete as wolffis ar With ougly*
> *ene and tuskis fer scherpare*

[There wild cats are as big as wolves are with ugly eyes and tusks far sharper].

Wolf – see **Oof**

Yowe – ewe. In the famous song by Robert Burns, *Ca the yowes tae the knowes* means *'drive the sheep to the hills'.*

Ca (from call) is used in the sense of drive or turn. So you can ca horses or a skipping rope or a handle.

A Scots version of 'one rotten apple spoils the whole barrel' is

> *ae scabbit yowe spyles twinty flocks.*

The yowe-trummle is a cold spell in early summer about the time of sheep-shearing, which would make the sheep shiver a bit.

Yowe or yowie is also used of a fir cone, from its resemblance to a curly-woolly sheep.

Zebra – zebra. This mammal does not occur in the wild in Scotland, which is just as well because in some dialects of Scots, the *Oxford English Dictionary* claims, the form *stripe* in this sense is unknown in genuine vernacular speech:

> *'strips' is the only word, e.g. for the stripes of a tiger or a zebra.*

However, zebras are found offshore, since zebra is a word used for the dog-fish.

There are not many large animals in Scotland. Most of them are useful to man in one way or another and are easily identified. Small animals come in a larger number of varieties but while many are common, a few are becoming quite scarce and some, like the polecat, are rarely seen.

3 Wee Beasts

And lat no small beistis suffir skaith [harm] na
skornis

This quotation from William Dunbar, writing at the beginning of the sixteenth century, makes him sound like the father of nature conservation. In fact it is a tactful suggestion to his monarch in *The Thrissel and the Rose* that his subjects should be compassionately ruled.

Backie, bawkie – bat. The most common variety of bat in Scotland is the tiny pipistrelle. The next most common variety is the long-eared bat. It is easy to identify; the name gives it away. You may see a Daubenton's bat, skimming over water, or a Natterer's bat with its pale underside. Other kinds of bat are rarely seen in Scotland.

Baudrons – hare, cat. See also **Bawd**, **Bawtie**, **Maukin**. The primary meaning of *baudrons* is 'cat' but there seems to be a tendency to extend words for cat to include the hare. Puss is another example of this.

Bawd – hare. Bawd bree is hare soup.

Bawtie – means a rabbit, but, confusingly, it has often been used in the past for the name of a dog. See also **Baudrons**, **Bawd**, **Maukin**.

Foumart – polecat, ferret. See also **Whitrat**. Foumarts were once hunted for their fur and there was formerly a market for hare, rabbit and polecat skins in Dumfries.

Sadly, there are not many polecats left in the wild, but the word is frequently applied to ferrets, especially ones of polecat colouring. A foumart cat has brindled fur. To *dae the foumart* is to be engaged in shady dealings.

Grey Squirrel – there appears to be an oblique reference to the grey squirrel in *A Dictionary of the Older Scottish Tongue* in a Latin quotation dated 1331. The quotation refers to *pure,* which, the dictionary tells us, is the belly fur of the grey squirrel. This is puzzling, since the grey squirrel is native to North America, a place which was not, according to many authorities, discovered until 1492. The grey squirrel was first released in to the wild in the nineteenth century and is a common sight in Edinburgh parks, where they live on a diet of mutton pies and egg sandwiches.

Hedger – hedgehog. See **Hurcheon**.

Hurcheon – hedgehog. The Mrs Tiggywinkle image was not current in Older Scots. William Dunbar (1508) likens the gait of his fellow poet Kennedy to the ungainly walk of a hedgehog:

Hard hurcheoun, hirpland [limping], *hippit*
[stiff-hipped, walking unevenly] *as ane harrow*.

He used the hedgehog for another unpleasant image in the *Twa Merrit Wemen and the Wedo* for the rubbing of a rough old man's face against a young woman's cheek:

With his hard hurcheone skyn sa heklis he my chekis.

This mark of affection is also referred to as a 'bairdie' and is not universally welcomed by Scotswomen, who, frankly, would rather have chocolates.

Witchcraft, as a result of which *Jonett* [Janet] . . . *wes trublit with hurchouins*, is documented in Pitcairn's *Criminal Trials* during a trial in 1591.

The Outer Hebrides are also troubled with hurcheons, which are not native to the islands but were introduced by gardeners to tackle slugs. Escaping into the wild, they have started to interfere with the local ecology through such antisocial activities as stealing puffin eggs.

Harry Hurcheon is the name of a dance in the North of Scotland, known elsewhere as *curcuddie*, which, according to Robert Chambers' *Popular Rhymes* (1847), is

performed in a shortened posture, sitting on one's hams, with arms akimbo, the dancers forming a circle of independent figures.

Lavellan – water shrew. This rarely seen but beautiful little creature is larger than an ordinary shrew, with black fur on its back and a paler underside. Like most shrews, they can be extremely fierce. They are very susceptible to pollution in the streams, ponds and reedbeds they frequent.

Leprone – young rabbit.

Mappie – pet name for a rabbit.

Maukin – hare. See also **Baudrons. Bawd**, **Bawtie**. Hares are surrounded by superstition and nobody is more superstitious than fishermen. Dougal Graham demonstrates this in a quotation from 1779 in his *Collected Writings* (1883):

> *Maukens are most terrible, and have bad luck,*
> *none will go to sea that day they see a Mauken, or*
> *if a wretched body put in a Mauken's fit [foot] in*
> *their creels, they need not lift them that day.*

John Galt in *The Steam-boat* (1822) tells of a commonly held superstition:

> *It is . . . believed . . . that the witches are in the*
> *practice of gallanting over field and flood, in the*
> *shape of cats and mawkins.*

If *the maukin is gaun up the hill*, business is prospering.

Mertrick – pine marten. There are pine martens in the Highlands with smaller isolated populations in Southern Scotland.

Moose – mouse. One of the best-known literary mice is the *wee, sleekit, cowrin, tim'rous beastie* rendered homeless by Robert Burns and his plough. Other notable mice feature in Robert Henryson's retelling of Aesop's fables in *The Tale of the Vplandis Mous and Burges Mous* and the *The Tale of the Paddock and the Mous*.

Mountain hare – this is found in both Scotland and Ireland, but the Irish ones do not turn white in winter as do the ones in Scotland where their winter camouflage is excellent, although this advantage may be lost as global warming reduces the snowfall even in the mountains of Scotland.

Moup, mouppie – familiar name for a rabbit. See **Mappie**.

Mowdiewort, mowdiewarp, moudie – mole. They make a famous literary appearance in *The Twa Dugs* by Robert Burns:

Wi' social nose whyles snuff'd an' snowkit;
Whyles mice an' moudieworts they howkit.

Puddock – frog; toad. Puddocks are much celebrated in Scottish literature. *From the Frogs of Aristophanes* translated into Scots by A. L. Taylor we have a vivid account of

> *. . . the rummle and the whummle*
> *O the puddocks as we tummle*
> *Doon the drain in the Rain!*

Again based on Greek, we have Aesop's fables elaborately retold by Robert Henryson and, in *The Tale of the Paddock and the Mous*, we see the paddock through the mouse's eyes:

> *Hir runkillit cheikis and hir lippis syde,*
> [Her wrinkled cheeks and her hanging lips]
> *Hir hingand browis and hir voce sae hace*
> [her hanging brows and her voice so hoarse]
> *Hir loggerand leggis and hir harsky hyde*
> [her loose legs and her rough skin].

Frog spawn, **puddock cruds** or **croots,** had uses both medicinally as a remedy for gout:

rub yer fit [foot] *wi't, an a' the time ye'r rubbin't*
keep sayin – Paddick cruds and snail broo;
Confoond the deil an cure the goo [gout]

(R. DE B. TROTTER *Galloway Gossip* 1901)

and for long-term weather forecasting:

Gin the puddock croot be at the lip o' the stank
[ditch], *it'll be a weet spring*

(*Buchan Observer* 22 August 1950)

Ratton, rotton – rat. Sermons in Scottish kirks have a certain reputation for being long and tedious and are admirably described by the Scots word *dreich*. The minister referred to in Robert Wodrow's *Analecta* (1702) might not have been best pleased when *In the midle of the sermon, a ratton came and sat doun on his Bible*, but no doubt all the small boys in the congregation were highly delighted. *Rotton* appears in many street names, including the alliterative Rotten Row, in recognition of the number of rodent residents.

Reid squirrel, ridd squirrel – red squirrel. The shrinking distribution of the red squirrel in Scotland is giving cause for concern and naturalists are working hard to ensure the survival of these delightful creatures. *Gleg as a squirrel* is a very apt simile for someone who is quick and agile either physically or mentally.

Shearmoose, sharemoose – shrew *Sorex araneus*. The name shearmoose is similar in sense to the English name 'harvest shrew' because it is disturbed when cereal crops are cut or sheared. The shrew has quite a few other names in Scots. Some, like **nebbit moose** [mouse with the nose] or **rone-moose** [mottled or reddish mouse – its back can vary from black to reddish-brown] refer to its appearance. Others, like **skrow** or **strow**, reflect regional pronunciations. The name **thraw-moose** derives from the superstition that if a shrew ran over your foot, it could paralyse or deform it. [Thraw means to twist or deform.] The smallest mammal in Scotland is the pygmy shrew, *Sorex minutus*, at only 5 grams in weight.

Weasel, wheasel – weasel. The weasel is one of several animals, including the stoat and the ferret, that are sometimes referred to as futtrats but in spite of the confusion in names, it is easy to tell the difference between a stoat and a weasel: a weasel is weasily distinguishable and a stoat's stoatally different. The *wh* spelling in wheasel reflects the Scots aspirated sound which has survived in Scotland since Anglo-Saxon times, although it has now been lost in England. It sounds a bit like *hw*. This form may have derived from an association with wheezle (similar to the wheezles and sneezles suffered by Winnie the Pooh's friend, Christopher Robin) because of the hissing noise a weasel makes when cornered.

Whitrat, futrat, whitterick – weasel; stoat; polecat; ferret. See also **Foumart.**

This word can be applied widely to members of the mustelidae family and so the definition given by John Burel in *The Passage of the Pilgremer* (1590) is still a good catch-all:

The quhittret . . . Ane litill beist of lim and lith And
of ane sober schaip.

The name literally means 'white rat' and is therefore
very apt for the stoat in his winter coat.

Another version of the 'hair of the dog' as a
cure is described by Dr Gilbert Skeyne in *Ane breve
Descriptioun of the Pest* (1568):

*As the quhittrat beand hurt be venome of serpent
seikis & eittis thairof.*

The smaller the animal, the more dangerous it is. The great
Clydesdale horse is a gentle giant but the shrew might
paralyse your foot. To study Scottish mammals, you need
to visit the countryside in winter as well as summer, to
see the stoat in its ermine coat and the mountain hare in
its white camouflage and, if you are weary walking over
hills and heaths, you can always stop and gaze restfully
into a river pool or loch for more wildlife watching.

4 Freshwater Fish

The sun glints over Neidpath Fell,
  And lights the forest grey ;
The dewdrop glistens on the grass,
  The cock proclaims the day.
Then up, my lads ! cast care aside,
  Throw business to the deil;
We'll fill our baskets frae yon stream
  That winds by Ashestiel.

> Let others toil frae day to day,
> This warl's gear to win,
> Or seek in pleasure's vain pursuit,
> For joys they ne'er can fin;
> But gie to me my weel worn creel,
> My ain rod in my han ,
> And tho' I'm poor, I envy not
> The noblest in the lan'.
>
> (Songs of the Edinburgh Angling Club)

Whether you are a fly fisherman filling your basket from the River Tweed like the angler in the song, or a scientific dipper with a net and a jam jar, there are hours of sport and fascination in Scotland's inland waters.

Baggie, baggie minnow – a kind of large minnow.

Beard(ie), baird(ie) – three-spined stickleback.

Beardie-lotchie, bairdie-lotchie – the loach.

Doctor – a large minnow; the red-breasted minnow.

Guddle – to catch fish with the hands, often by groping under stones or the banks of a stream. This is surprisingly a latecomer to the language, being first recorded in the early nineteenth century. Further research is clearly required into the vocabulary of early poaching methods in Scotland.

Katie beardie, Katie bairdie – loach. This Katie is only very distantly related to the young farmer of the children's song:

> *Katie Bairdie had a coo, Black an white aboot*
> *the moo, Wisnae that a dentie coo? Dance Katie*
> *Bairdie!*

Peen-heid – the young fry of the minnow or stickle-back. Literally meaning 'pin-head', this is a splendidly graphic term.

Powan – powan *Coregonus clupeoides clupeoides*. This

is a Scottish variety of the freshwater houting found in Loch Lomond, Loch Eck and the Carron Valley reservoir. It is a protected species.

Reid gibbie – stickleback.

Salmon, saumon – salmon. Scotland is famous for its salmon rivers. Salmon fishing was once a thriving industry and great salmon stake nets were a familiar sight on sloping sandy beaches. The fish were also caught in cruives (wicker containers) and netted from boats. In some places such as the Solway, large rectangular haaf nets were used by fisherman who waded out and held the net in the current of the estuary. Salmon farming is taking over as a safer way of supplying the current enthusiasm for salmon, but it is only a century ago that servants were complaining about being fed too much salmon.

Sodger – the red-breasted minnow.

Troot – trout. Perhaps less glamorous than the salmon

in the eyes of many fishermen, the trout, whether grilled or smoked, has a lighter, more subtle flavour than salmon.

Vendace – *Coregonus albula*. Although this fish is common in lakes of northern Europe, it is only found in two lakes in England and in two lochs in Scotland.

Having explored the fish of lochs, burns and rivers, let's move downstream to the salt water of the firth [estuary] and out to the sea.

5 Sea Life

Wha'll buy my caller herrin?
Tho some folk ca them vulgar farin
Wives and mithers maist despairin,
   Ca them lives o men.

(Lady Nairne)

Some of the strange fish names are the result of fishermen's superstitions. Mentioning the fish by name was a sure way of not catching any. Most of them are very geographically limited so please do not go to a fishmonger and ask for a blacksmith!

Baffert – porpoise. See also **Pellock, Puffy**.

Baggit – (of a fish) full of spawn.

Barra bramble – a jocular name for jellyfish, after the Isle of Barra.

Beggerman – flounder.

Blacksmith – halibut.

Blin-ee – dogfish (literally, blind eye).

Bonnet fleuk – brill.

Buckie – whelk. Boil them and eat them with a pin.

Clunkertonie – jellyfish. *Clunker* and *tonie* both refer to the stinging effects.

Cod – perhaps because of its commonness and its economic importance, a huge vocabulary has built up to describe cod at various stages and in various conditions. Add regional variation into this kedgeree and you have half a dictionary. Some of the choicest terms include the Shetland word **Scots-Willie** for a young cod. A **shingler** or a **soosler** are Caithness words for a thin, badly nourished cod with a big head. A **ware-cod** or **maroochan** is a poor cod at the start of the season. Cod have been air dried without salt as **stockfish** since at least the thirteenth century and these dried cod are sometimes called **wind fish** in Kincardine because of the method of drying. Other regional words for cod are **droud**, **killine**, **kleg**, **pullach**, **ruggie**, **purr**, **slink** and **stuckie** to name but a few.

Colmie – coalfish. Also known as the **sellock** or **sillock** or **piltock** when young, or the **smoolyer** in Avoch (pronounced Och) which had a quite distinctive dialect of its own. The adult fish are known as **seths** or **saiths** or graylords.

Fleuk – flounder.

Gipsy – herring pilchard.

Glut – the slime on a fish.

Gurnard – also known as the **crooner** or **windy sparl** [rectum] from the sound it makes when taken out of the water. Other names include **gowkmey**, **noud**, **oof** [wolf], **crodan** and **captain**, although these may no longer be current.

Heevil, haivel – conger eel. This name goes back to *haf,* an Old Norse word for sea. It also appears in Modern Scots as eve-eel and evil eel but these, in spite of the wicked appearance of this fish, are clearly related to *haf.* See **Yaa, yaw.**

Herrin – herring. The herring, the silver darlings, were once a mainstay of the Scottish coastal economy and the success or otherwise of the drave or annual herring fishery meant comfort or hardship for many families. The young women from fishing villages would travel to the main landing places where they would gut the herring and pack them in salt.

Lapster – lobster.

Mattie – a young maiden herring with the roe not fully developed. These are the tastiest ones.

Mere-swine, meerswine – porpoise (literally sea-pig). The nineteenth-century lexicographer, John Jamieson, tells us:

> *As a vast quantity of fat surrounds the body of this animal, it has given occasion to the proverbial allusion, 'as fat as a mere-swine'.*

Muldoan – basking shark.

Orca – sightings around northern Scotland are becoming increasingly frequent. Orcas have even been known to make the occasional rare foray into the Firth of Forth.

Partan – edible crab. Borrowed from Gaelic, and recorded in Scots texts from the fifteenth century, the word *partan* has got its claws well and truly into the Scots idiom. Early usages seems to mean any kind of crab but, later, partan usually denotes the edible crab. In the *Foulis Account Book* of 1700, we find that a luxurious dinner of *lapster and partans and brandie* cost £2. 18. 6, but, less extravagantly, William Alexander in his 1871 novel *Johnny Gibb* writes of *bawbee partans*. A halfpenny would have been all that a *partan-fisted* or miserly person would have willingly paid. A *partan-back* was used in times past to refer to a soldier, the colour of the crab resembling the tunic of a redcoat. A *partan-taed* person walks with in-turned toes. A *partan-faced* individual is not a pretty sight and if you really dislike someone you could call them *a partan-faced sculduddery loon* – a colourful phrase from John Carruthers' *A Man Beset*. *Fu as a partan* meant full to the brim, as in a quotation from James Stewart's *Sketches of Scottish Character* (1857):

> He had primed his *proboscis* [with snuff] *till it was as 'fou as a partin',*

and it is easy to imagine the *little man, as full as a partan of buttoned, brushed, and powdered pride* described by Henry Farnie in *Fife Coast* (1860).

Gaining renewed popularity with gardeners is the partan-hoe, a cultivator with curved claw-like prongs. The *Aberdeen Press and Journal* of 21 April 1953 tells of the availability of *Round Shovels, Dung Graips; Dutch, Draw and Parton Hoes.*

Even when its insides are picked clean, the partan has its uses. Small children made partan-cairties, pulling the shells along on a string, and the claw could be used as a pipe in which dried leaves of coltsfoot or 'shellaggie' (Latin: *tussilago*) was smoked as a substitute for tobacco.

Pellock – porpoise. The harbour porpoise is Scotland's

most common cetacean and you are particularly likely to see it off the north-west coast. See also **Baffert**, **Puffy**.

Piltock – a coalfish around its second year. This word, used in Orkney, Shetland and Caithness, has an interesting derivation. It comes from Old Norse *pilt* meaning a young boy and to that is added the diminutive suffix *–ock*.

Podlie – young coalfish; pollack.

Puffy, puffy-dunter – porpoise. So called because of the puffing noise they make when they surface. See also **Baffert**, **Pellock**.

Saith, seath – mature coalfish. *The Description of the Countrey of Zetland* from the second half of the seventeenth century gives a somewhat fanciful origin of the name Shetland:

> *By the Scots & English it is called Shethland, because in old time there were many sheathfish caught about its coast.*

It is certainly true that seath have been an important part of the diet of Scotland for centuries. The same volume records that they *are very beneficial by reason of the oyl they make of their livers*. This mouthwatering serving suggestion comes from *The Orkney and Shetland Miscellany* edited by Alfred and Amy Johnston:

> *Saide-an-gree was the saith boiled with its liver till the oil floated on the water. When the fish was dished the 'gree' was skimmed off and poured over the fish.*

Sand eels – the *Dictionary of the Scots Language* contains a quotation which seems to suggest that the Charlie Chaplin film, in which he eats his shoes, might have something to do with a Scottish recipe:

> *The greatest dillagate* [delicacy] *ava'* [of all] *Was sandells fried wi' bacon.*

Fortunately, this is only an alternative spelling of sand eels.

Scalder, Scowder – a large venomous jellyfish. So called because its sting seems to scald the skin.

Seal, selch, selkie – seal. When conditions were hard and food was scarce, seals were a valuable source of nourishment and there are many accounts of mass slaughter of seals in former times. Sir Robert Sibbald's *The Description of the islands of Orkney and Zetland* (1633) explains:

> *Upon the west side of the bay there lye several rocks, or skerries, which selches frequent in the moneth of November, and the inhabitants neglect not to wait upon them to kill them, the skins they sell, but the bulks they salt, and in time of Lent, they eat them as sweetly as venison.*

Nevertheless, perhaps because of the hauntingly human expression in a seal's eyes, a large body of legend has grown up around these mammals, some based on shape-changing powers. One of the best known is the subject of the ballad of the Selchie of Sule Skerry:

I am a man upon the land;
I am a selchie on the sea,
And when I'm far frae every strand,
My dwelling is in Sule Skerry.

As this legend tells, the selchie is not above fathering children who are then taken back to the sea.

Sillock – young coalfish. They have a fine liver of which the Shetlanders used to make pies.

Spoot – razor-clam. Best fried or stewed in milk. Their presence in the Household Books of James V of Scotland suggests that they were even fit for a king in 1525:

Spouttis, bukez, solis, podlois

[spoots, buckies, soles, podlies or razor clams, winkles, sole, coalfish.]

Swithers – dried-up jellyfish. If you are handling nets, they irritate your eyes.

Whale, whaal – whale. It is not so long ago that Scotland was a whaling nation, as the name **whale-eaters** for natives of the town of Dumbarton reminds us. The most commonly sighted whale around Scotland is the minke whale. If you are very lucky, you might see a humpback whale or a fin whale.

Whale-bubble – jellyfish.

Yaa, yaw – conger eel. See **Heevil**, **haivel**.

Zebra – the smooth hound or dog-fish *Mustelus vulgaris*.

We have looked at birds that fly, mammals that walk, run, climb or jump and fish that swim, but we have kept the best for last. Now we are ready to move on to that wonderful collection of creatures that creep, crawl, slither and scuttle.

6 Creepy Crawlies

Frae ghoulies and ghaisties and lang-leggity baisties
and things that go bump in the nicht, may
the guid Lord deliver us.

(Traditional)

Long-legged creatures, short-legged creatures, many-legged creatures and creatures with no legs at all are much less terrifying when they become familiar. This chapter is therapy for the arachnophobe, food for the insectivore and guaranteed to have you itching as you read.

Adder, edder, ether – adder. This and other snakes are supposed to have been chased out of Ireland by St Patrick. There are no adders in Orkney and Shetland either, but St Patrick does not get any credit for this.

An etherstane or adderstone is a small, perforated prehistoric stone or bead used as an amulet. J. Leyden in *Minstrelsy of the Scottish Border* (edited by Sir Walter Scott 1802) explains:

> *The adderstone, among the Scottish peasantry, is held in high veneration . . . the name is applied to celts, and other round perforated stones – The vulgar suppose them to be perforated by the stings of adders.*

Ant – Scots names for the ant include **Emock**, **Emmerteen** and **Pismire**.

Gresshopper played aw simmer lang,
Lowped aboot and strummed his sang.
Whan winter cam he sang nae mair;
His wame wis toom, his cupboard bare.

He gaed tae see the ant, whase store
Wis spillin ower wi treats galore.
Says 'Spare me just a bite eneuch.
I'm findin life a wee bit teuch.'

Says she, 'Whit did ye in thae days
Whan food wis free in parks and braes?'
I sang the newest sangs frae France.'
'Weel,' says the ant, 'Awa and dance!'

(ROBINSON after AESOP and LA FONTAINE)

Bee – it is the custom, when a member of the family dies, to go down to the hives and whisper the bad news to the bees. At one time, the bees were then put in mourning with black ribbons being tied to the hives. In some of the Southern states of America, including North Carolina, the bees are told of a family bereavement.

Beetle – Black beetles in general are known as **clocks**, **clockers** or **cloakers**. A **Bum-clock** is a humming beetle.

Berry bug – harvest mite.

Bike – the nest of wild bees or wasps, sometimes also applied to the nests of other insects, such as ants. It can even be extended to a crowd of troublesome people. In both 1605 and 1636, collections of criminals were referred to as *an infamous byke of lawles limmars*. In Banff in 1695, some of John Leel's children were accused *of holling a bees' byke . . . in tyme of sermon.*

Bumbee – bumblebee.
   As I gaed doun
   The stackyaird dyke

I stuck a stick
In a bumbees' byke.

Sic a stishie
Sic a steer,
Sic a bizzin
Did I hear.

I got stang
Frae a big bumbee,
And Jings! that stang was sair.
Never will I
Herrie a byke
Gif I leeve for evermair.

(J. K. ANNAND)

Bum clock – see **Beetle.**

Butterflee, butterie – butterfly. The Deil's butterflee, or butter deelie, is the tortoiseshell. The French butterflee is the common white.

Centipede – this multi-legged minibeast has almost as many names as it has feet, including **Jennie-hunder-feet**, **Jennie-mony-feet**, **Meggie-mony-feet**, **Jeck wi' the monie feet** and **Forty-fittit Janet.** Its dancing skills and the tragic results of trying to analyse what comes naturally are recorded in the famous song *The Wee Kirkcudbright Centipede* by Matt McGinn.

Cleg – horsefly.

Clocks, clocker, cloaker – see **Beetle**.

Crane fly, daddy-lang-legs, Jennie-lang-legs, lang-leggit-tailor, Peter-lang-shanks – daddy-long-legs, cranefly. As irritating as the adult can be, fluttering around the bedside light, the young is even more of a pest. Known in north-east Scots as a **torie**, it can do considerable damage to crops. It should be noted that this word comes from Gaelic *toran* 'the borer' and bears no etymological relationship whatsoever to any similar-sounding political supporter. There is a helpful reference in James Arbuthnot's recommendations for treating the soil (1735):

> That destructive animal called the Tory . . . If the
> soil be inclined to tory-eat, it should be turned over
> as soon as possible after frosty weather.

Earwig – there are probably more names for earwigs in Scotland than for any other creature. They include **clipshears**, **collieglean**, **callanglean**, **forkietailie**, **hornie gollach**, **gollacher**, **geelog**, **gullack**, **gullachan**, **gavelack**, **scotchiebell**, **scodgible**, **switchpool** and **twitchbell.** Many of these are very localised.

> The horny golloch is an awesome craitur,
> Souple and scaly.
> He has twa horns and a hantle o feet
> And a forkie tailie.

Emmerteen – see **Ant**.

Emock – see **Ant**.

Ettercap, nettercap – spider. This old name for a spider appears in English as attercop. Atter or etter is suppurating matter, so this is not a very pretty name. The form nettercap comes from a confusion of word division in *an ettercap*. A similar thing has happened, in the opposite direction, with the modern English word *adder* and Scots word e*ddir* which derive from an earlier form, *nedder*.

Ettercap could be applied to a person with a poisonous disposition.

See also **Spider**, **Wabster**.

Flech, flae – flea. *Flechin* means fidgetting as if you had flechs. *Kill-the-flechs* is another name for feverfew. An unusual way of getting rid of people you don't like is suggested in Pitcairn's *Criminal Trials* (1610):

> I vow to God, yf I be not quyte of him, I sall putt
> ane fleche in his hoise [stockings].

Flee – fly. This is somewhat confusing for the non-Scot. A rhyme often chanted by children goes:

Ane, twa, three,
Ma grannie couched a flee.
She sauted it and peppered it
And had it tae her tea.

Granny oobit – a hairy caterpillar. See **Oobit.**

Hairy grannie, hairy oobit, hairy worm – a hairy caterpillar. See **Oobit**.

Jennie-mony-feet – see **Centipede**.

Kailworm – the caterpillar of the large white and small white butterfly. Literally 'cabbage worm'.

Keb, ked – tick. This loathsome little arachnid is found on sheep and deer and is easily picked up by dogs or humans among the heather or bracken. Henry Stephens in *The Book of the Farm* (1889) observes:

During summer and autumn sheep are subject
to attacks by the 'maggot-fly' . . . and to become

infested with various parasites. Chief amongst the latter is the 'ked,' 'keb,' or 'sheep-tick.'

Their partiality for human blood is well attested. William Cleland in *A Collection of Several Poems and Verses* (a1689) suggests a lack of personal hygiene:

Their swarms of vermine and sheep kaids,
Delights to lodge beneath the plaids;

but even this is surpassed for sheer gothic horror by a poem (1874) by John Hogg on the Siege of Roxburgh:

While up his thighs, wi' devilish bustle
Ran mony a ked;
Now they hae lost their gume [bite] *and gustle* [hearty meal],
Sin' Robin's dead.

Ticks are potentially dangerous as they may carry Lyme's disease, but risk can be minimised if they are removed cleanly as soon as possible and people who are diagnosed early are usually successfully treated. So be sure to tell your doctor about your tick if you become unwell up to 30 days after a tick attack. Always inspect yourself carefully after a day in the hills. Do not just rip them off or you risk leaving mouth parts embedded (theirs!). Try rotating the tick gently in an anticlockwise direction, holding it as near its head as possible. They will also drop off if immersed in oil.

Leddy launners – ladybird.

Leddy, Leddy Landers,
Leddy, Leddy Landers,
Tak yer cloak aboot yer heid
And flee awa tae Flanders.
Flee ower the firth and flee ower the fell;
Flee ower the pool and the rinnin well
Flee ower the moor and flee ower the mead;
Flee ower the livin; flee ower the deid;
Flee East; flee West;
Flee til him that loes me best.

(Traditional children's rhyme)

Mauch, mauk – maggot. W. D. Cocker warns in *Further Poems* (1935):

> *A smittle [infectious] thing the mawk, Yae [one] flee [fly] contaminates a flock.*

Once the flock has become infected with maggots, it is said to be *maukit*. In John MacTaggart's *Scottish Gallovidian Encyclopedia* of 1824, one example reads:

> *The sheep grow mawket on the hill, And sair themsells they claw*

and if you are feeling sorry for the sheep, help is at hand in another of W. D. Cocker's poems (1932):

> *Shorn yowes were marked wi' keel, Mawkit anes got doctored weel.*

Mauk itself is probably Scandinavian in origin, and although not frequently recorded in medieval Scottish literature, there is a reference to 'mauch muttoun' (maggoty mutton) in William Dunbar's poem *The Flyting of Dunbar and Kennedy*, written sometime before 1508.

Maukit can be extended to anything or anyone that is particularly filthy and disgusting. In the *Dictionary of the Scots Language*, one quotation from 1986 reads:

> *A friend of mine decided to wash his bike the other day cause it was mockit.*

And the word may also be associated with childhood reminiscences, as in the following example from the *Herald* in 1993:

> *"My God, yur mockit, mockit, the fulthiest laddie I've ever seen" she would shriek, as she roughly rearranged the tousled ginger carpet above a face as filthy as the Earl of Hell's waistcoat".*

Midge, midgie – midge *Culicoides impunctatus*.

You can get to like Scotland's climate. Many people prefer it to the climate anywhere else. In fact, there is a good side to almost everything in Scotland – except the midgie. Although it is only the female midge that bites, there seems to be a disproportionate number of them. Worst at dusk in sheltered places, they make beer gardens a no-go area for those unfortunate individuals who are particularly attractive to this Scottish curse. Top tips:

- do not go out unless it is either blowing a gale or pouring rain (no problem there);
- wear light-coloured clothing;
- apply repellant liberally, the oilier the better.

The midges, the midges,
I'm no gonnae kid ye's,
The midges is really the limit,
Wi teeth like pirhanas, they drive ye bananas,
If ye let them get under yer simmit! [vest]

(ANON.)

Moosewab – spider's web.

Oobit – caterpillar. Any caterpillar that looks like a short piece of wool qualifies as an oobit (woolbit). Hairy oobits are usually the caterpillar of the tiger moth. *Medical History* (1825) refers to a remarkable cure:

When a boy, ill of Hooping-Cough, his mother,
for the cure of that disease, tied round his neck a
number of 'hairy oubets', sewed up in a piece of
cloth – and with evident success.

Pismire – see **Ant**.

Schell padocke – 'shell-toad', tortoise. *The Register of the Privy Council of Scotland* (1565) describes a penny on one side of which was a crowned palm tree with *ane schell padocke crepand up the schank* [trunk] and King James VI of Scotland refers to *The slow-past* [paced] *shelpaddock* in one of his poems.

Slater, sclaiter – woodlouse. John Jamieson in his *Etymological Dictionary of the Scottish Language* (1825) suggests a cure which may be worse than the affliction:

The heartburn, or Cardialgia. The common cure for
it, in the country, is to swallow sclaters, or wood-lice.

Slow-worm – *anguis fragilis*. This harmless legless lizard can be seen in the summer months in rough grassland or moorland. Drystane dykes [drystone walls] provide handy shelters where they can soak up the sun. Like other lizards, they can shed their tail when they feel threatened.

Sodger – ladybird. So called because of the soldier's red coat.

Spider, speeder – spider. Killing a spider is supposed to bring bad luck:

> *Gin ye want tae live and thrive*
> *Let a speeder rin alive.*

However, keeping a spider in captivity could be good for the health; a letter from Sir Robert Moray to the Earl of Kincardine (1658) recommends as a cure for fever:

> *Put a great spider into a box made of 2 wallnut*
> *shells and hang it about the neck so as it may be*
> *about the slot of the breast.*

See also **Ettercap**, **Wabster**.

Spurrie – a rove beetle, any staphylinid beetle which moves very fast, such as earwigs, silverfish, etc. **Lang spurries** are centipedes and millipedes.

Torie – see **Cranefly**.

Wabster – weaver, spider. Literally a weaver, wabster was extended to the spider for its webmaking skills. John Galt makes a reference to a spider wabster in *The Entail* (1823):

Down came a spider wabster as big as a puddock.

Worm – worm. In Older Scots, a worm could be anything from an earthworm to a dragon. As late as 1590, Pitcairn's *Criminal Trials* describes a case where Bessie Roy was charged, amongst other heinous things, with drawing a circle on the ground, making a hole in it and,

be thy conjuratiounes, thow causit ane grit
worme cum fyrst out of the said hoill, and creip
owre the compace.

She was found to be innocent.

In James Somerville's *Memorie of the Somervilles* (1679), he describes

Ane hydeous monster in the forme of a worme soe called . . . by the country people (but in effect hes been a serpent, or some such other creature,) in lenth three Scots yards, and somewhat bigger then ane ordinary man's leg, with a head . . . in forme and cullour to our common muir edders.

By this time a degree of scepticism about dragons seems to have crept in.

However, you can still see dragons in Scotland today. Just look at the foot of the Apprentice Pillar in Rosslyn Chapel and there, sucking at the roots of the stone vegetation which decorates the column, is a circlet of little dragons. As the Earls of Rosslyn have strong connections with Orkney and, hence, with Norway, it is likely that these little dragons are a reference to Niðhogg, the dragon of Norse cosmography, who lurked under the earth feeding on the roots of Yggdrasil, the world-ash.

Earthworms were once held to be of great therapeutic value and in Dalyell's *The Darker Superstitions of Scotland* (1647) you can read how, all for the good of its health,

A child being stripped was rubbed with the oyle of wormes [and] held over the reik of a fyre.

A worm-web is a spider's web. James Hogg describes a chilly night:

My bed-clothes consisted of a single covering not thicker than a worm-web.

A *worm in the cheek* is toothache but a cure is at hand. *Notes & Queries* (1854) states that, in Orkney,

toothache is by the country people called 'The worm', from a notion they have that this painful affection is caused by a worm in the tooth or jawbone. For the cure of this disease, the . . . charm, called 'wormy lines', is written on a slip of paper.

This could be the answer to the current shortage of National Health dentists in Scotland.

Epilogue

I hope this little ramble through the Scottish countryside has inspired you to get out and about armed with binoculars and perhaps a magnifying glass – certainly with plenty of midge repellent. If you attempt any of the animal-based medicinal remedies suggested in this book, we absolutely deny any responsibility for such rash action on your part. All sightings of Nessie should be reported to the proper authorities.

As to the riddles I quoted earlier in this book, here are the answers in case you got stuck:

Riddle

The laverock and the lark,
The bawkie and the bat,

> *The heather-bleet, the mire-snipe,*
> *How many burds be that?*
>
> (J. MacTaggart *The Scottish Gallovidian Encyclopedia* 1824).

Answer

The answer is two. A laverock is the same bird as the lark. That gives one bird so far. The bawtie is the same as the bat – and that, of course, is not a bird at all. The heather-bleet is the same bird as the mire-snipe. So the total is TWO.

Riddle

> *Hey-up ma cuddy,*
> *Ma cuddy's ower the dyke,*
> *And if ye meddle ma cuddy,*
> *Ma cuddy'll gie ye a bite.*

Answer

Ma cuddy is a stinging nettle.